Love Presenting

Hate ([illegible]ed)

Powe[illegible]oint

CONTENTS

DO THE OPPOSITE OF THE MANY

1. **Fewer** PowerPoint slides.
2. **Less** waffle.
3. **Shorter** sessions.
4. **No** late starts.
5. **Fewer** coffee breaks.
6. **No** distractions from time-wasters.
7. **Clear** actions at the end.
8. And notice how people **love your presentations...**

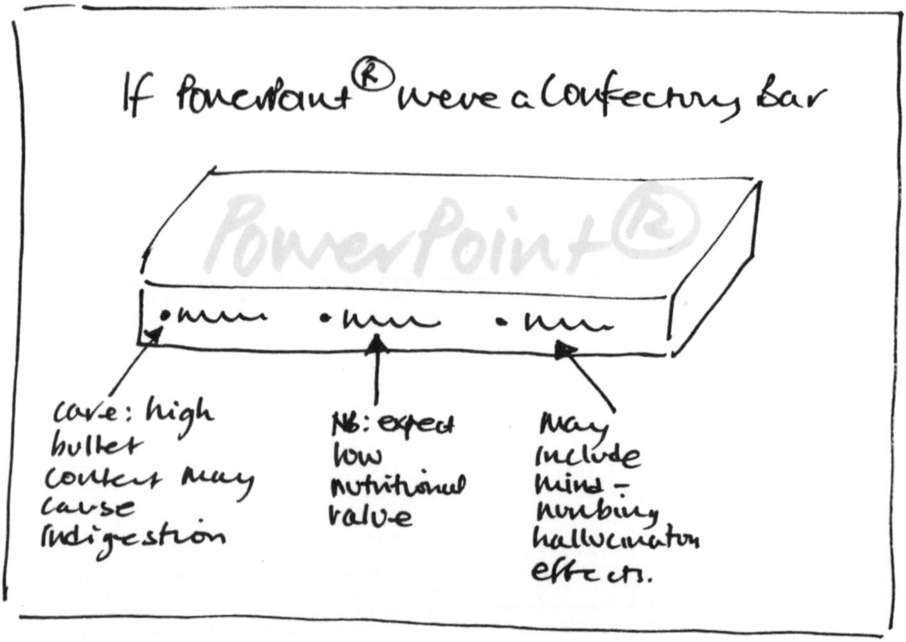
If PowerPoint® were a Confectionery bar
PowerPoint®
care: high bullet content may cause indigestion
NB: expect low nutritional value
May include mind-numbing hallucinatory effects.

WHAT WENT (BADLY) WRONG? 1

All presenters should be professional. They should be prepared. They should help their audience understand the messages that are being expressed. That has been so since the start of time when tribal histories were shared and battle plans were explained around camp fires.

In addition, those new to the business of standing up in front of a collection of people have always sought anything which can help reduce their nervousness – a large part of which comes from worrying that they won't remember what they are meant to say – also, since the beginnings of time.

Put these two factors together and you create the temptation for presenters to put their words up in front of people on a 'slide'. After all: it helps you remember what you need and want to say and apparently helps the audience, too (although more on that, later). But Old World of Work Technology (chalk-boards, overhead projectors, acetates) made that hard work and expensive. So slides and words-on-slides were kept to a minimum, until a few decades ago when PowerPoint was invented.

And before we consider the impact of that invention, let's add an additional important factor: as the rate of change in business increases, the requirement to have more people briefing more people about more things, accelerates, so more presenters are on their feet more of the time.

PowerPoint meant that words on a slide became cheap and easy. And the continuing New World of Work rate of change has changed 'presenting' from

SEVEN QUICK FIXES FOR AN INHERITED SLIDE DECK

Much advice for presentations and use of PowerPoint assumes we have total control over the presentation and/or we are building it from scratch. In fact this is often not the case. Here are some tips if you have to use or deliver someone else's presentation and you would like to make it better.

1. Build in some unplugged i.e. bits where you don't use slides/ technology. An easy one is to delete the agenda and summary slides and just speak those from memory.
2. Replace sentences with key words so that you add value rather than reading a script.
3. Replace one or two slides with e.g. a picture or a quotation.
4. Create an interaction part: a simple exercise which encourages involvement.
5. Ensure every slide is simple.
6. Delete logos apart from the title slide; they are a distraction.
7. Practise delivery a couple of times: a good rhythm can really rescue a poor presentation.

something only those skilled in their craft do, into something all and sundry are expected to carry out. Mix the two together and you get PowerPoint Paralysis: do what everybody else does: put your words on a slide, read them out and joke (embarrassingly) about it.

You're reading this book because you've had enough of that state of affairs. You know there is one, and only one, reason for doing a presentation: to get action. And PowerPoint Paralysis is not the way. That's not to say PowerPoint (and of course similar pieces of software) do not have their use: they certainly do.

We're going to restore the joy of attending a presentation and re-discovering what it is to present with passion. We're going to remember that there is a reason for having the very expensive gathering of people in that room: it is to get people to do something. And finally we're going to remind ourselves there is a very thin line between chaos and creation in a presentation.

WITH CARE, YOUR PRESENTATION WILL...

1. Create intimacy with the audience through your use of space and story-telling.
2. Keep the message simple through analogy, facts and direction.
3. Keep focused on the core message through examples and interaction.
4. Illustrate that you are the person adding value. It was 'worth coming today'.
5. Only allow the audience to move at the pace you decide.
6. Show your skill in not resorting to an 'auto-prompt'.
7. Allow ultimate flexibility.

The Rosetta Stone
now available =
in Powerpoint

PRESENTING UNPLUGGED 2

The big aim in this volume is to re-establish the concept of a 'personal presence'; this we will define as the way a presenter 'is' or the fact that his/her communication comes through their state (their energy and manner), coupled with their use of space and of appropriate story and structure.

We are NOT saying there is anything wrong with slides nor in particular PowerPoint. A good slide can make a presentation; PowerPoint in particular enables very complex ideas to be simply and easily communicated. And ironically that is why the recent fashionable habit to ask presenters to 'not use PowerPoint' or 'use no more than three slides' is not more helpful when trying to create the very best presentations. It simply changes the problem.

No, instead we will take you through seven key concepts which when applied will make you an amazing presenter. Each one is straightforward. Each–applied well–would be enough. Put a few or all of them together and you can create something stunning.

REDUCING NERVES BEFORE A PRESENTATION

is less a presenting issue and more a time management challenge. The more times you can rehearse the fewer the nerves. Practise enough and you can get those nerves to the **perfect point**: enough to keep you agile and quick thinking but not so much as to cause you to be distracted and forget points. *How many times is enough?* Only you can decide but certainly with new materials schedule three run-throughs and notice how significantly better you feel on 'take 3'.
Never present live without rehearsal, however brilliant your notes.

THE POWERPOINT RADICAL

So you **love PowerPoint**. That's fine. Try some of these more radical ways of using it:

1. Just have one slide for the whole of your presentation. Start with one item on the slide and as you talk and unfold your points build the slide. On departure give people a copy of the complete slide. Do not give them a copy as you present.
2. Have slides, but make them all images no words.
3. Have slides, but make each a single number which is the foundation of your point.
4. Be minimalist: get rid of all the clutter and logos etc.
5. But above all, be different. The 'pattern interrupt' of doing it differently will help get your point across.

THREE REASONS WHY YOU NEED TO BECOME AN OUTSTANDING PRESENTER

3

Given the threshold that has to be reached to become one of the very best communicators, some decide to never start the race. They avoid presentations. They mumble from notes. They read from a sitting position. No. No. No. It'll catch up with you, it really will. The ability to present is strongly associated with your leadership skills, your credibility and your sheer drive. Thus: decide to become a great presenter. Here are the reasons:

1. It's the only real way to get fast concrete action. If you want action from a group of people, get them in the room with you. That way you can look them in the eyes, ask for what you want, answer their questions, create a project plan and MAKE IT HAPPEN. No other way is as fast, responsive, engaging and simply pragmatic. And that is of course why you are doing it!
2. You'll be measured by your ability to do it. This may or may not be fair. But those who can stand up in front of a group of people and inform/enthuse them, tend to get noticed and therefore it's a skill you need to get really good at. This is of course true in your daily job but also in interviews.
3. It's the best personal development course on the planet. Every time you stand up, you are on show, arguing your case, handling difficult people, managing time, attempting to meet an objective. And that's just for starters. You'll learn a heck of a lot about yourself as you progress, if you are willing to do so.

Arrggh!

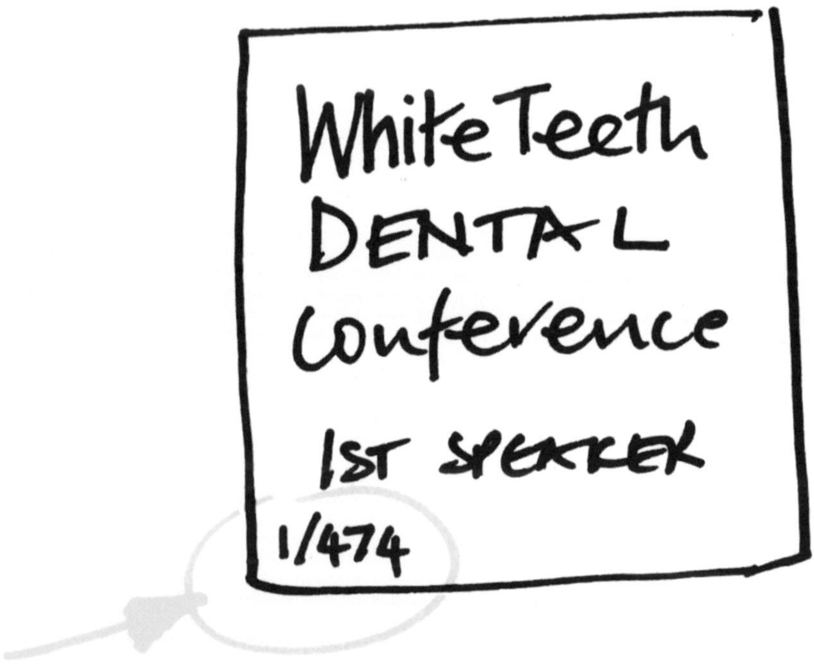

FOUR PROVISOS 4

The following four points are helpful to bear in mind as you decide to 'step up' your presenting career.

1. **No failure only feed-back**. So the presentation went badly. Some difficult questions, you over-ran and at one point there was some down-right hostility. You feel: 'I failed'. No: you didn't. You actually got considerable, accurate feed-back for making it even better next time. Learn from it.
2. **Love the dip, love the plateau**. This is a great quote from author George Leonard. He reminds us that when we are learning we often appear to get 'stuck' i.e. cease improving. Your story-telling just doesn't seem to be improving. Keep practising: it will. You can think of this as consolidation or being on a plateau. Then there are those times where we get worse before we get better; this is re-wiring. You don't use as many PowerPoint slides and understandably you find it more difficult to manage time. You'll soon get the hang of it. Don't resist either situation: plateau nor dip, simply see them as steps on the path: go with the flow.
3. **What does this situation say about me?** Audiences can absolutely, definitely irritate us. But if they do, we must always ask: what could I be doing to make things better? Let's be honest: are we simply boring? Have we very simply been intimidating? Did we get the wrong brief? We cannot win every presentation. But if we own our communication, if we genuinely believe it is our responsibility to make it as easy as possible for the audience to understand then we will get our messages across.
4. **I'm only here for the action!** But above all, you are taking people's time. They could be doing something else. Respect that time and drive to action.

HOW TO THINK LIKE A POWERPOINT PRESENTER

1. OK. 1h. That's 120 slides.
2. Let's see what old decks I've got that I can cannibalise.
3. Get the text smaller. Get more bullets. Hence more value.
4. Get ALL my words on; don't want to forget anything.
5. Cool quotation from Michelangelo. Everyone has quotes. Not sure what it means.
6. Embed a current film clip. Should wake them up.
7. Joke about PowerPoint being a bit dull. But do it anyway.

THE BIG SEVEN, NUMBER ONE: STATE OR YOUR STATE IS THEIR STATE

5

THE BIG IDEA

It's you. It's not the slide nor the embedded video nor the opening joke. Those can contribute. It's you. It's emanating from your very pores. It's your presence in that room. It shows in how you move. Your expressions. How you hold yourself, your flow, your energy. It's your being, your state, your passion for the whole project. You've heard it so many times: *'his/her enthusiasm was infectious'*. In fact any mood is infectious. A boring presenter will make an audience bored. A cool, calm dedicated presenter will get an audience to treat a subject with appropriate gravitas.

Here's the thing: you must **be** *the state you want your audience to acquire.*

THE BIG TIP

When you are planning your presentation (BTW: we're going to do that properly in the section on 'storyboarding'. For the moment just know that we will have a planned presentation), there's a key question and a resulting follow-up you need to ask and get a clear answer to:

1. What state (energy/attitude/mood) do I want my audience to be in?
2. So: what does that say about me?

Archaeologists were excited to find the first PowerPoint slide.

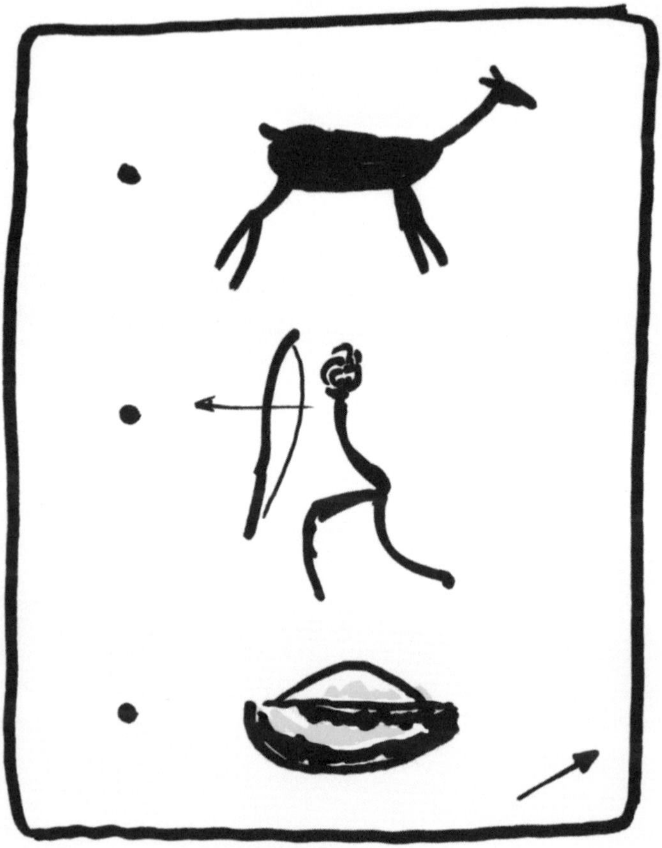

THE BIG SEVEN, NUMBER ONE: STATE OR YOUR STATE IS THEIR STATE

5

HOW TO DO IT

The state most people want most of the time is to be energised and 'up'. And they find that difficult because as they get close to the presentation they become more nervous and anxious, the exact opposite of what they want. Here are some practical tips for accessing a great state of 'bring it on, I'm ready':

1. Newspaper. Take a rolled up newspaper. Find somewhere quiet and bash that newspaper across the back of a chair for 90 seconds. I defy anyone to not feel energised after that. (I know. I know: you're thinking that is daft. See 'the surgery is open' below).
2. Decisions. Make a decision to be up-beat. Walk that way (shoulders back, head high). Talk that way (variation, pace). Look that way (appropriately dressed for action).
3. Thinking patterns. Don't focus on what might not work. It's too late for all of that. Block negative thoughts by just saying (internally) 'next thought', 'next thought'.
4. Connect with old times. As your presenting career builds you'll be able to flood your mind with an increasing numbers of good experiences. Remember one or two. Or three.
5. Reverse engineering. This is an extension of point 2: you know how a great presenter looks and sounds. So do exactly that.

SEVEN PRESENTATION STRATEGIES YOU CAN BORROW FROM THE BEATLES

1. Tell a **story**. *She's Leaving Home.* Make it engaging and sensory-rich.
2. Be **local**. *Penny Lane.* Connect to the audience in the room, not just any audience.
3. Give **hope**. *She Loves You.* Present a solution, whatever the problem.
4. **Surprise** them. *Maxwell's Silver Hammer.* Present well, but not predictably especially for repeat performances.
5. Provide the **simplicity the far side of complexity**. *Let it Be.* Add value, not just more PowerPoint slides.
6. Have **energy**. *Drive My Car.* Wake them up and get them thinking.
7. **Less is More**. *Across the Universe.* A total philosophy in 3.47. That's a great goal to have.

THE BIG SEVEN, NUMBER ONE: STATE OR YOUR STATE IS THEIR STATE

5

THREE EXAMPLES

1. Fantastic new product launch: your state needs to be up-beat, excited. So: bash that newspaper, leap in the air and listen to rock music before going on stage.

2. Redundancies announced and many are going to occur in your team: you are about to speak to them. Your state needs to be calm, respectful, empathetic with gravitas. So: take some time out, get 'busyness' out of your head: walk around the block. Think what it must be like to be told you have just been made redundant. Now stand tall and act 'can do'. Be empathetic but tell it as it is.

3. Weekly team meeting: your state needs to be empathetic but action based. Exemplary but encouraging. So: plan it well, turn up with great energy but be willing to drop that energy and hand it to others around the table.

THE SURGERY IS OPEN

1. Q: Err, bash a newspaper? That's silly. *It is. And that's partly why it works. Stop complaining, give it a go and see how it helps.*

2. Q: The culture around here is very 'moderated'. I'm not sure how well it would go down if I turned up with some real 'bounce'. *Well: find out. I think you'll be amazed at how many people come up to you and say 'loved your session'. Try it.*

3. Q: I'm sorry. Sometimes, I simply don't always feel like talking to people. Surely that's just human. *It sort of is. Which is why we make a distinction for those people we call 'professionals'. A professional does what is necessary even when they don't feel like doing it. Respect your audience.*

... through the use of PowerPoint Einstein had not only explained the relativity of time but demonstrated it. The 30 minute presentation had seemed like days.

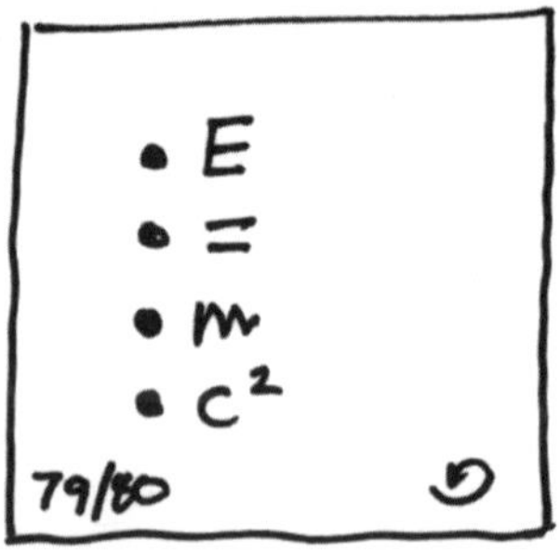

THE BIG SEVEN, NUMBER TWO: SPACE OR INCREASE THE POWER; CHANGE THE INTIMACY: MAKE IT YOUR WORLD

6

THE BIG IDEA

Many speakers simply accept what is given to them for their 'space'. They walk into a tiny over-heated room. Or a steeply-raked lecture theatre. A room with no windows. Arrggh: this could spoil so much of their message. The space, you see, is your–and their–world for the 1h meeting or the two-day workshop. It is crucial to see or at least get a detailed specification and/or visuals of the room you will be in so that you can make use of the space to best effect in order to maximise the power of your message. The wrong or mis-used space can ruin it.

Your 'presenting space' whether chosen or imposed has an impact on two factors:

Firstly, the magnitude or strength of the message. Imagine speaking from the lectern. Now imagine coming out from behind the lectern and walking into the audience. Have a different effect? You bet it would.

And secondly the intimacy, the connection you achieve with the audience. Imagine pacing the room for a while. Now sit at the table with the team. Soften your view and look them in the eyes and say: it's over to you now... Powerful? Exactly.

These two factors are of course strongly inter-related.

TTD (THINGS TO DO): TO USE POWERPOINT CORRECTLY

Use PowerPoint to:

1. Amplify a point e.g. with a graph.
2. Allow internalisation e.g. have a quote, but don't read it aloud; simply allow audience to read it.
3. Boost internal visualisation e.g. picture of complex impenetrable jungle when talking about 'tough markets'.
4. Show a process unfolding e.g. how technical problems are resolved schematic.

Don't use PowerPoint:

1. To act as your teleprompter. Write a script if you wish, but don't put it on a slide-deck. Just have 'markets' rather than 'markets are getting increasingly tough every year'.
2. Simply because everyone else does: learn how to present 'unplugged'.
3. To provide notes for the audience. Do that in word and provide it as a handout for later distribution.
4. to allow people to read your story before you have said it.

Start to use PowerPoint correctly.

THE BIG SEVEN, NUMBER TWO: SPACE OR INCREASE THE POWER; CHANGE THE INTIMACY: MAKE IT YOUR WORLD

6

THE BIG TIP

When planning, ask the questions:

1. What degree of volume/impact do I need?
2. And for the connection I want with these people, what intimacy do I need?

HOW TO DO IT

Imagine two axes each of which has three points. The first is the vertical axis on which you have three options:

1. Top of the axis is *standing*. Standing with shoulders back and weight equally distributed across your hips; this is the leadership position. It says: 'for the moment, I am in command'.
2. Middle of the axis is *the 'perch'* or sitting on the edge of a table or perhaps the back/arm of a chair. This is deferring some of your responsibility to the group: '*so what do you think?*', you say as you perch. But notice what you can do if you start to lose control to someone who is going off at a tangent... Right, quickly return to standing position.
3. Bottom of the axis is the *sitting* position. Here you are totally deferring to the group. Maybe sitting down with them to share your views.

The final slide of the gunfight at the O.K. Corral

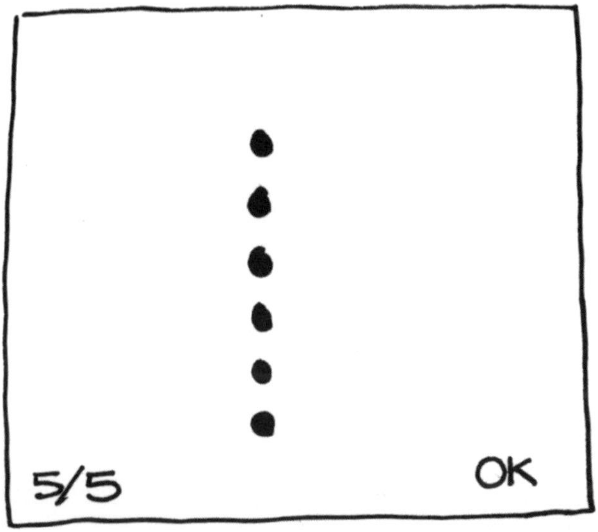

THE BIG SEVEN, NUMBER TWO: SPACE OR INCREASE THE POWER; CHANGE THE INTIMACY: MAKE IT YOUR WORLD

6

The second is the horizontal axis on which again, there are three options:

1. The most formal: *behind the podium*. This is a very detached position and is generally not recommended. Even if you are speaking at a conference, resist it: come out from behind the forum and connect with your audience.
2. Which brings us to *the stage*. This is an area immediately in front of your audience. Being in this area allows manoeuvrability, connection and responsiveness.
3. *In the audience*. This is essential as the audience gets larger and larger. Go present from the back of the room, between the aisles... In essence remove 'the back rows'.

A good 'default' position is leadership + stage.

THREE EXAMPLES

1. Team meeting. Seriously consider holding the meeting in different locations. The 'same old' room can create an association with 'same old' thinking.
2. Product launch at which perhaps, sadly lots of antipathy is expected. Make sure you have a roving mike. Get a soap-box to stand on. Go present from the back of the room after the initial introduction. Present from wherever you can and bring the whole audience into your thinking.
3. Half-hour key-note at the sales conference. Get off the stage. Get the audience standing and doing things.

THE PRESENTATION SURGERY IS OPEN

Yeah–the reason I'm back is I've been following the 'less PowerPoint' mantra and YES I'm enjoying it more and YES people are clearly more engaged in what I am saying but now I have problem with those who want a complete record of what I say... in the 'old days' I could just give them a copy of my PowerPoint slides. What do I do?

Firstly–good news on breaking out of PowerPoint and glad to see that broadly the new approach is working. Let's step back a minute. When you present you actually need to provide for three variants on the main stream of communication:

Variant 1 = what you are going to say. Effectively your notes, not for public display.

Variant 2 = what you will show to the world e.g. a slide, a prop.

Variant 3 = your handouts. The record you might like them to take away.

And of course that is why many people use PowerPoint – it does all three of these functions in one–but badly.

A suggestion. Write your 'script', then turn it into your public presentation. Then create an 'executive summary' in say word and make it available at the end of the presentation either as a hand-out or perhaps a down-load via your blog. Hope that helps.

THE BIG SEVEN, NUMBER TWO: SPACE OR INCREASE THE POWER; CHANGE THE INTIMACY: MAKE IT YOUR WORLD

6

THE SURGERY IS OPEN

1. Err, what's the difference between a Presentation vs. Meeting? *Once upon a time they were quite distinct entities but with the advent of PowerPoint as a ubiquitous communication tool they have begun to merge. In many ways does it matter to try and define them? Simply return to the question: what is my outcome, here?*

2. Err, but surely some rooms are simply unsuitable and there's no other option? *True, but try and be creative. Maybe there's room in the canteen before it is fully set up for lunch-time? Maybe it's even better sitting in the reception area. Certainly don't let a depressing 'bunker' of a room cast a shadow over your otherwise great training session.*

3. Err, but what about rooms you've never been in before? *Rule 1: don't let it happen to you. Rule 2: if it does happen to you, get into the room early and re-arrange it as best you can. Sometimes, simply changing the orientation can have a beneficial effect.*

THERE'S A PATTERN TO SPOT

1. To get better at juggling: **practise.**
2. **To get better at closing the deal: practise.**
3. **To get better at writing: practise.**
4. **To get better at negotiation: practise.**
5. **To get better at presenting: practise.**
6. **To get better at gardening: practise.**
7. **To get better at Life: practise.**

If JFK had used Powerpoint

THE BIG SEVEN, NUMBER THREE: STORY OR STORIES ARE MEMORABLE; BULLETS ARE FORGETTABLE

7

THE BIG IDEA

Somewhere along the way we have shifted our way of teaching and inspiring from the saga to the instruction manual. Sagas are of course great stories which hold an abundance of ideas in an easily digested and remembered form as a consequence of the powerful connecting narrative. And importantly they are embedded with rich emotion. Emotion which gets people to feel an actual part of the topic rather than just disconnected and detached from it. When people are truly connected to the issue they are likely to wish to take action. Stories connect. PowerPoint so often distances and therefore makes it harder to get the action you so seek.

Instruction manuals on the other hand are really useful for interpreting raw data and realising steps in how to–for example – rebuild a fuselage.

There is of course nothing wrong with an instruction manual. In fact when you are committed they are brilliant. The problem is until someone is committed such a communication device can put them off. Too often the PowerPoint presented is the equivalent of an instruction manual.

A PRESENTATION TIP

Remove that which might distract from your message e.g.:

Stuff left on whiteboards and flip-charts which seems intriguing. Get rid of it.

Too obvious clocks, especially ones on the wall just behind you. Remove it during your presentation.

Left-over lunch. Wheel it into the corridor.

Blackberries. Just say NO.

Questions: decide what you want to do (as you go along/at end?) and stick to it.

Overly voluminous notes. Reduce and tidy.

Late arrivals. Try and ensure they enter from the back of the room, not front nor side.

That tie. Get rid of it.

THE BIG SEVEN, NUMBER THREE: STORY OR STORIES ARE MEMORABLE; BULLETS ARE FORGETTABLE

7

THE BIG TIP

When planning, ask the questions:

1. What action do I want of my audience?
2. How much do I need them to be engaged with this idea to get it to work?
3. How can I use a story to get them fully engaged?

If you realise that engagement needed is low then *maybe* you don't actually need them in the room; maybe the whole process can be carried out by e-mail or a couple of small group meetings? If you do need them in the room, then ramp up the engagement to get action.

HOW TO DO IT

Great stories are

1. Relevant. Don't just 'tell a story'. Dig one out from your own experience which shows that you e.g. understand what it is like to be starting at the beginning of your career in a large organisation where support can often be limited.
2. Have a clear 'point'. Keep the story 'complex' enough to be interesting but 'simple' enough that the point is clear. The complexity should come through characters and events. The point e.g. 'taking ownership' should shine through without doubt.
3. Just start. Don't say 'let me tell you a story'. Just start telling the story; the shift of pace is itself a way of holding attention (see 'spikes' later).

The PowerPoint Slide DECCA rejected...

and dropped in a bin.

THE BIG SEVEN, NUMBER THREE: STORY OR STORIES ARE MEMORABLE; BULLETS ARE FORGETTABLE

7

4. Your story wherever possible. Make the story yours. Better an 'ordinary' story that occurred to you than a more dramatic one which is borrowed or made up. It being your story allows you to remember it easily, answer questions about it and avoids you needing to be evasive if some asks 'did that really happen?'

5. Sufficiently detailed to make it interesting. Not *"I started at Global in the September"* but *"I remember the taxi dropping me off at reception on that wet September morning. Everybody seemed to have something else to do. Even the taxi driver commented..."*

6. Often structured bad news... good news... We are drawn to the bad news of others. So, start your story on a low and build to a positive result. *"So there I was, Christmas Eve morning, the phones ringing and my boss lying on the floor with acute stomach upset from too much drink the night before..."*

THREE EXAMPLES

1. Customer service conference. Avoid too many models, too many acronyms and too many statistics. Telling a few relevant stories will illustrate your concepts and turn abstract into concrete.

2. Team meeting. Flip the tables and ask them for their stories. Tell stories of productivity, of astonishing customer service or leadership.

3. Training course on health and safety. Get delegates to work in pairs and write a story which illustrates an excellent approach in dealing say with a severe burn victim. A great dramatic story reveals that those writing really understand the emotions involved.

4 X 4 PRESENTING

If you have ever been lucky enough to go on a proper 4 x 4 vehicle training day, I bet you loved the experience: you felt the bumps, you were so near the water some leaked in over the window top and you were sure you were going to roll on that incline. You were IN the experience; you felt exhilarated. You were not a detached observer. That's how a great presentation works: get them involved. Pull them in. Get physically close to the audience then tell them great stories and then be provocative and then... See the difference it makes.

Give them a 4 x 4 presentation. They get too many which just take the easy route from mid-town to down-town with a lot of boring stops at traffic lights and the same old scenery.

THE BIG SEVEN, NUMBER THREE: STORY OR STORIES ARE MEMORABLE; BULLETS ARE FORGETTABLE

7

THE SURGERY IS OPEN

1. Err, I'm no good at stories. *One word: practise!*
2. Err, that's all very well but I'm from the finance department. We are numbers, numbers, numbers. *And that's fine. But perhaps remember that when you are communicating to a non-financial audience the fastest way for them to understand what you are talking about is illustration. And one of the easiest ways to connect and illustrate at the same time is through a story.*
3. Err, how much detail should I use? How long should I go on for? *Listen to other presenters and note how they do it. If in doubt have more detail but talk for less time. If the audience stays with you then next time you can experiment with talking for longer if you need to.*

If Isaac Newton had used PowerPoint

THE BIG SEVEN, NUMBER FOUR: STRUCTURE OR WE ARE THERE TO GET ACTION. PERIOD

8

THE IDEA

Nobody ever talked to a group of people without wanting something. Barack Obama? *Elect me*. Winston Churchill: *stay believers in this great little island*. Your Health and Safety Rep: *stop leaving rubbish in stairwells*. Your teacher: *use the French Imperfect tense correctly*.

THE BIG TIP

When planning, ask the question: what do I want of my audience? As a consequence of my presentation what must they do differently?

HOW TO DO IT

Structure your presentation to lead to the action. Everything you do is for that purpose. Thus, there are seven steps:

1. **Wow**.
2. **Agenda**.
3. **Connect** with the audience.
4. Ask for what you want; **the solution**.
5. Take **questions**.
6. **Summarise**.
7. Ask for the **actions**.

TTD (THINGS TO DO) TO IMPROVE YOUR PRESENTATION SKILLS

1. Try something new.
2. Practise.
3. Get feed-back.
4. Try something new.
5. Practise.
6. Get feed-back.
7. Practise.

THE BIG SEVEN, NUMBER FOUR: STRUCTURE OR WE ARE THERE TO GET ACTION. PERIOD

8

LET'S TAKE EACH IN TURN

1. The **Wow** is the 'wake them up', 'show them that you are serious' stage. This is where you show that you have something to say, something valuable to offer, something which may well be useful for them. Here are some examples: "What I want to show you this afternoon is that by coaching our people we could grow this business by 22% without need for extra headcount"; "Ladies and gentlemen, not only is our software solution unique it is uniquely environmentally sound" It is also where you show that you are a professional, that you start on time and that your respect their time.
2. The **agenda** is brief and to the point. It is so that people can plan their time. And for larger audiences it is where you can 'cover off' any health and safety issues such as fire procedures.
3. The **Connect** is where you show the audience that you do understand their position, you do empathise, you do understand what is required of them. Examples and context etc. all keep coming back and relating to them.
4. The **solution** is where you discuss what you want them to do, your proposed way forward, your solution.
5. The **Q&A** is getting questions out of the way so that you can get a clear run toward your request for action.
6. **Summarise**. This is where you state what you want.
7. Then you ask for **action**.

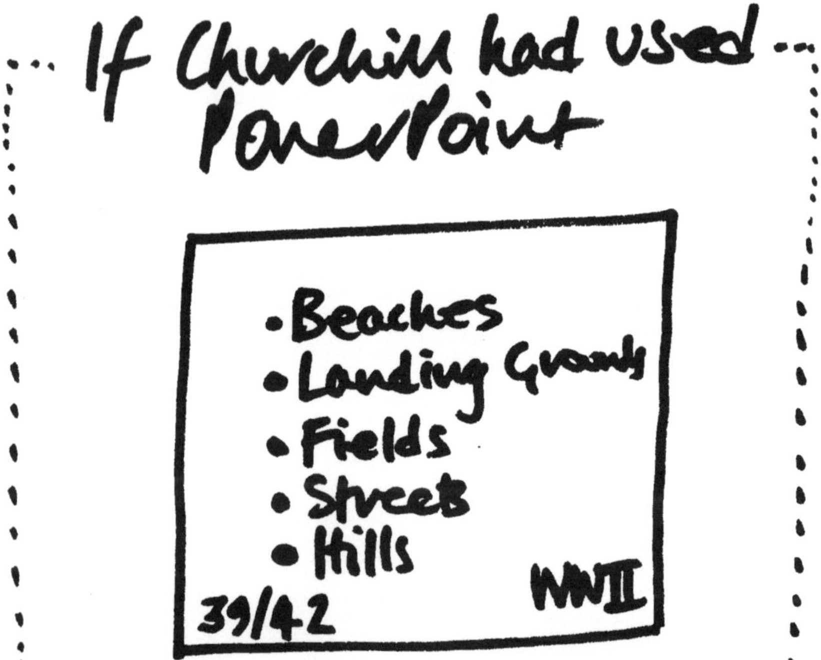
If Churchill had used...
PowerPoint
• Beaches
• Landing Grounds
• Fields
• Streets
• Hills
WWII
39/42

8 THE BIG SEVEN, NUMBER FOUR: STRUCTURE OR WE ARE THERE TO GET ACTION. PERIOD

THREE EXAMPLES

1. Headcount request. *So what you want from the senior management team is for them to approve your request for two extra heads. But you know that their thinking is in cost-cutting and saving money. Therefore you have to show that is what this extra head will do. Ultimately it will save money.*
2. Low team morale. *Team morale is low and needs to rise. You need to show that you understand their perspective, even if you do not accept it.*
3. Major sale. *You win the sale simply by showing you have a deeper understanding of the client's needs.*

THE SURGERY IS OPEN

1. Err., we set actions but they never seem to be followed through. *It is worth understanding the difference between an implicit action and an explicit action. An implicit action is a nod of the head: easily done. An explicit action is one where there is a detailed action as to the way forward. Insist on more explicit action while people are in the room.*
2. Err, there are simply too many people in the room to get actions. *This can be the case where you are executing a presentation to a large audience. In which case warn the audience that you will ask for team submissions, or ask one or two people from the audience.*
3. Err, as I plan my presentation I am unsure what the action actually is? *Point one: is there really a reason for the meeting? Could the whole topic simply be covered by a good e-mail? Point two: maybe you are having the meeting too early. Maybe you need to do more groundwork yourself to define the problem more fully.*

PINCH FROM THE MOVIES

To give your presentation extra impact, pinch from the films:

1. Start in the middle. Well, perhaps not right in the middle but definitely not at the start. Skip all the boring bits... you can trickle those in later... get right to the heart of the matter. Just like a good film does.
2. Change time. Films have flash-backs. So can you: switch tense and talk case studies and make them real. Just like the films do.
3. Have a car chase. Pick up speed. Get really fast. Nearly lose it, then return to the main theme. Just as in a good film.

Remember: you are a film director now. And your audience expects the best.

THE BIG SEVEN, NUMBER FIVE: SPIKES OR CHANGE=ENGAGE. ENGAGE=ACTION ACTION=MISSION ACCOMPLISHED

9

THE BIG IDEA

We are designed to be distracted. Why? Because it's all very well sitting around the camp fire, enjoying stories and fresh mammoth steaks but if nobody hears the rustling in the bushes, they could well be susceptible to an ambush. Hence our tendency to be alert to any possible fleeting noise, activity or wandering thought. So what's the solution?

- Replace the external 'distractions' with your own more valuable distraction: if what you are saying is very engaging then the noise of an ambulance going by on the road outside at high-speed will hardly register.
- Reduce the time and space for external distraction. Keep your session short. Keep the pace moving. And don't use a conference room over-looking the conference swimming pool.
- Maximise everything we have talked about so far. Multiply great state by a great story by a great story by...

If CTU insisted Jack Bauer used PowerPoint in the field

THE BIG SEVEN, NUMBER FIVE: SPIKES OR CHANGE=ENGAGE. ENGAGE=ACTION ACTION=MISSION ACCOMPLISHED

Thus in a typical presentation, we can get a graph of attention vs. time appearing which looks very much like this:

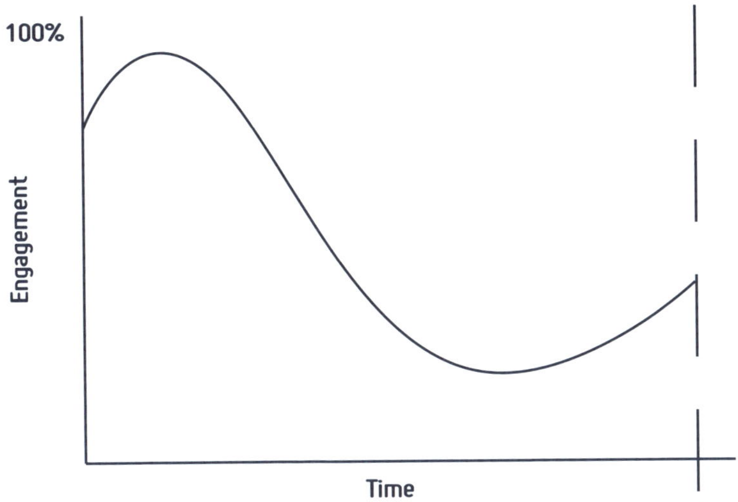

THE BIG TIP

Start with the essential premise that 'less is more' i.e. that the less time people are having to 'concentrate' the more likely that you will be able to hold their attention for the full time; in particular there is less time for their own self-generated distractions to appear. Always question long periods of time; why has an hour been set? Simply because it is a handy unit of time on the schedule? Then return to the fundamental questions:

30 MINUTES BEFORE YOUR BIG PITCH TO 30 PEOPLE

-30. Get into the room. Pace. Get the feel. Walk to the back.

-29. Sort the temperature as best you can. Remember: it will get warmer.

-28. Remove distractions. Stuff left on white-boards. Yesterday's sandwiches.

-27. Load and check your slides.

-23. Adjust the furniture as best you can to get the audience as 'intimate' as you can.

-19. Ensure you have a flip-chart for impromptu stuff.

-17. Practice your opening three minutes, twice.

-11. Check your clothes.

-10. Get a bottle of water: have a sip.

-9. Walk tall. Breathe easily.

-6. Greet first arrivals. Smile and raise your energy.

-2. Scan and check all OK. Say 'We'll be starting in two'.

-1. Close the door.

0. Start with a bang (and do not acknowledge late-comers until later).

THE BIG SEVEN, NUMBER FIVE: SPIKES OR CHANGE=ENGAGE. ENGAGE=ACTION ACTION=MISSION ACCOMPLISHED

9

1. What do I need to get across or more accurately, what action, what changes do I need to get out of these people in my audience, my room?
2. Given 1, for how long do I need to talk?
3. How intrinsically interesting is this topic? There is a difference between bonus news and health and safety issue, between redundancy and...
4. What's been happening before my session?
5. What happens after my session?
6. What's the environment like. Too hot/cold/noisy etc...

HOW TO DO IT

Of course, you are already aware of:

1. State: a state which is appropriate for the session will hold people's attention.
2. Space: changing space and making good use of space will maximise their focus; help everyone to feel they re on the front row.
3. Story: the right story will 'centre' people and spot the mind drifting.
4. Structure; a clear structure will neatly pull people from one point to the best.

To which let us add:

PRESENTING BREAKTHROUGH SEVEN

It's not just about...

1. Your solution, it's a lot about their challenges.
2. Fill the time available, it's a lot about giving excellent value.
3. Having fun, it's essential there is action.
4. Impressing them, it's certainly about making it easy.
5. Look-alike clone PowerPoint slides, but relevant visuals which help.
6. Blaming the small size of the room, it's a lot about taking ownership as presenter.
7. 'Giving a presentation', it's about developing an awesome skill.

THE BIG SEVEN, NUMBER FIVE: SPIKES OR CHANGE=ENGAGE. ENGAGE=ACTION ACTION=MISSION ACCOMPLISHED

9

5. Question, real. A question directed at a member of the audience e.g. 'so. Tim, what would the savings be for your team?' Remember the purpose is to create a sense of energy and involvement not one of fear of being embarrassed. When you ask a real question they must be able to answer...

6. Question, rhetorical. A rhetorical question causes a peak in interest through the change in tone, the expectant pause, the constant tugging at the audience. The change from statement to question gets the audience thinking.

7. Props. There is a general principle to replace the abstract with the concrete. A prop or real physical thing is an ideal way to do this. For example, it's tricky for most people to really get their head around what a million pounds worth of savings really looks like or means. So convert it into real money. Cut up scrap paper, rubber-band it and put some real banknotes on the top. Or convert it into a number of training days. Or...

8. Anecdotes > jokes. A quick anecdote or joke can work well. But ensure it is relevant otherwise we move into stand-up. And be sure to run it by someone; in a world of political correctness you might find that some are unhappy.

9. Voice. Another general principle is the one of being unplugged. You, yourself can do a tremendous amount without needing any support at all.

10. Media changes. Hi-tech media changes are of course very popular at the moment e.g. an embedded video. These do work but sometimes something very low-tech such as a the use of as flip-chart to explain some numbers is useful.

A GREAT POWERPOINT SLIDE

1. **Cannot be read ahead:** it needs your interpretation.
2. **Doesn't distract** from your message.
3. **Complements** what you are saying.

Such slides are rare which suggest *we need fewer than we generally create*.

THE BIG SEVEN, NUMBER FIVE: SPIKES OR CHANGE=ENGAGE. ENGAGE=ACTION ACTION=MISSION ACCOMPLISHED

9

11. VFT or Value For Time. Ensure every minute is valuable to those in the room. Then they will stay interested.

THREE EXAMPLES

1. Team meeting. *Three easy ways to hold attention: (1) change the 'chair' i.e. who runs the meeting every week. (2) change the order of the agenda every week (3) ensure everybody knows in the room they will be called upon to contribute at any time.*

2. Training course. *Two easy ways to hold attention: (1) have a good strong pace to the sessions (2) make it 100% relevant.*

3. Major conferences. *Three easy ways to create better sessions: (1) insist on rehearsal with feed-back (2) ask for minimum PowerPoint (3) shorter sessions*

THE SURGERY IS OPEN

1. Err, what do you do if you are definitely 'losing it' i.e. they are simply not interested. *You have three options: (1) accept that it is a very dull topic and/or there is a lot of hostility to what you are talking about; get through it and when you finish, reflect on what you might have done differently (2) stop the presentation and be bold and ask the audience what you should be doing differently. If you can make that change, do so. If you can't, explain that and finish as professionally as you can and learn for the future (3) stop the presentation and examine what went so fundamentally wrong and never let it happen again.*

How to be an instant Guru.

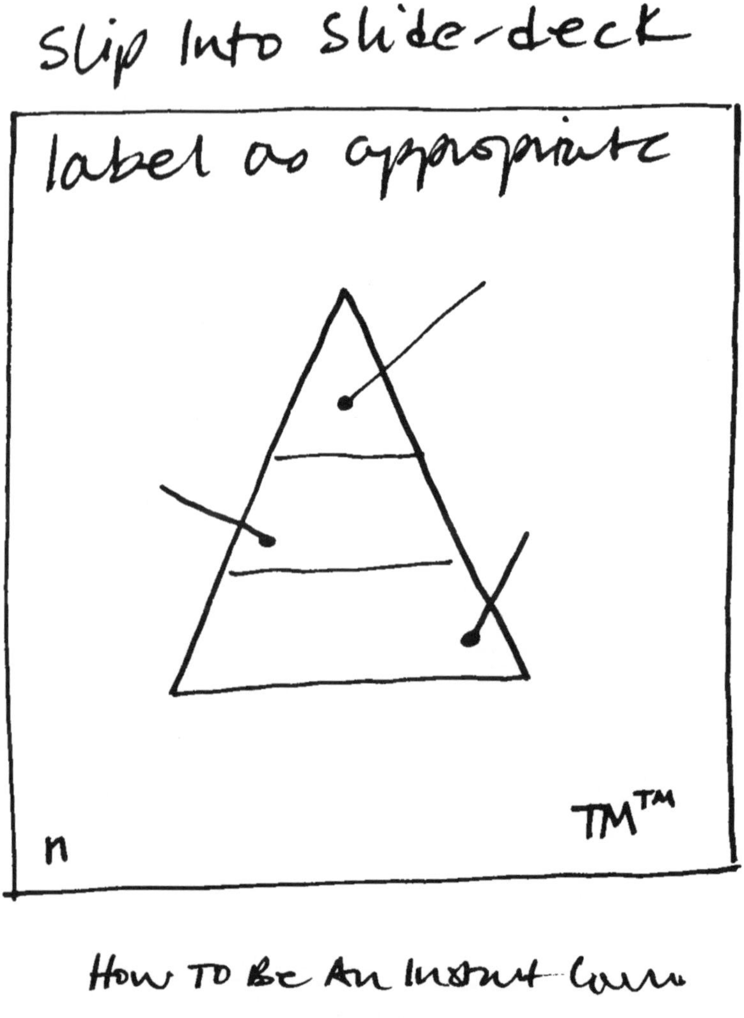

THE BIG SEVEN, NUMBER FIVE: SPIKES OR CHANGE=ENGAGE. ENGAGE=ACTION ACTION=MISSION ACCOMPLISHED 9

2. Err, What about making more use of 'exciting' visuals and music. *Because they're so frequently used they are not in fact that exciting any more. Just as 'flashy' PowerPoint has become ubiquitous, so have embedded videos... You will create better spikes by something more 'ordinary'.*

3. Err what about ordinary day-to-day meetings which can become mind-numbingly dull? *Ask whether they do need to be a meeting or whether in fact it could simply be a briefing sheet, then reduce the time and finally share the responsibility for making it 'more interesting'.*

NINE THINGS NOT TO SAY IN YOUR PRESENTATION

1. The colours looked at lot better at 1.30 am this morning.
2. We are experiencing a paradigm shift in customer expectations.
3. I'm standing in for the guy who really knows what he's talking about.
4. There's probably too much on that slide.
5. I realise I will run over on time by about 20 minutes.
6. Arrggh... so you don't have an extension cable?
7. Does anyone know how to get rid of that on the screen?
8. So, you've actually heard all of this before? Yesterday?
9. My wife chose this tie.

THE BIG SEVEN, NUMBER 6: STORYBOARD OR YOU ARE A FILM DIRECTOR

10

If you have been reading this book sequentially you will realise that a good presentation has a lot 'happening', even though the audience will have (should have) no idea about all that you are doing: using spikes, managing flow and visuals, remembering content, hitting time goals, answering questions, resisting interrupts, keeping the audience involved, reaching your own objectives... A good presentation is complex, even if you are speaking for just 10 minutes. In fact, it's just like a great film which involves a couple of car chases, a café scene and a walk along the beach with many interleaving 'ordinary' scenes: if it is a great film we simple see a great film, a great thriller not a collection of individual shots. So with your presentation. It needs variety, it needs pace, but it needs to be 'a whole'. Hence the story board.

THE BIG TIP

Let's say you are planning a 15 minute presentation to an audience of 35 senior people. Draw a matrix – a sort of giant Excel spreadsheet – four by four to give you sixteen boxes. Each 'cell' represents a minute of time (with one spare, of course). Into each cell you can now capture both what you <u>want</u> to say but also <u>how</u> you wish to say it. What you need to say is already dictated: you know that you will work though wow/agenda/connect/solution/questions/summary/action. The story board allows that to be captured but more importantly it also dictates how those sessions will be run.

London Tube Map in PPT Format

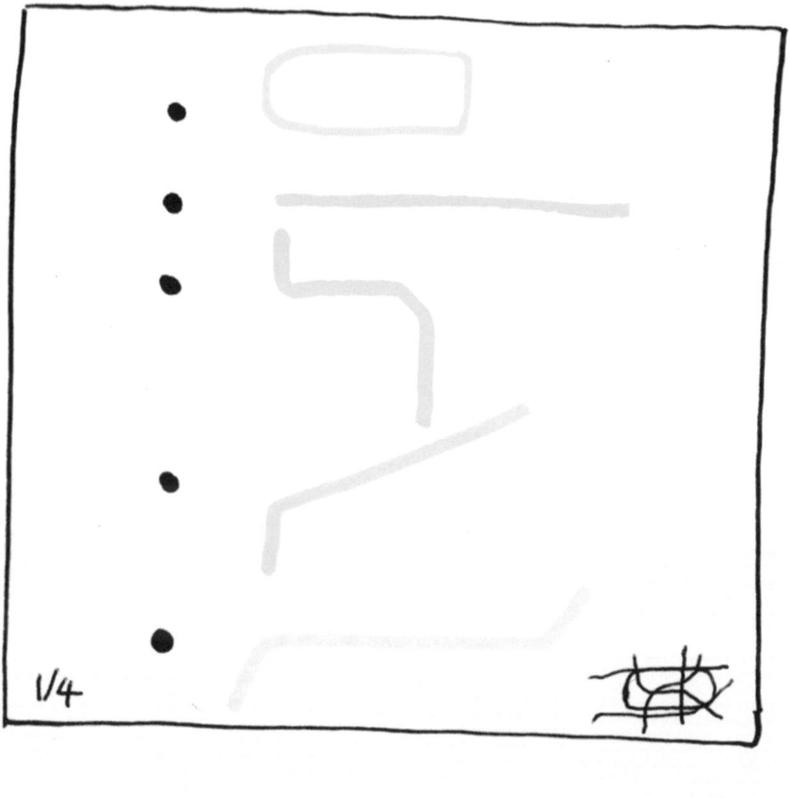

THE BIG SEVEN, NUMBER 6: STORYBOARD OR YOU ARE A FILM DIRECTOR

10

HOW TO DO IT

Stage One

Take each section of your what i.e. wow/agenda/connect etc. and consider how you want to present that. Thus your wow is to get across how shocking the current levels of customer service are. That's your what. So, how do you get it across? Well you might show a short clip of a video. Perhaps you have a story. Maybe you could gather some experience from the audience and get them interacting. Decide which is your preferred approach. A 'top tip' is to put these 'whats' and 'hows' onto 'yellow stickies' which means that you can re-plan more easily (see next stage).

Stage Two

Once you have complete the matrix i.e. every 'cell' is completed with a what and a how, stand back and consider whether your presentation has sufficient flow and variety. Maybe it's very 'pacy' at the start but then loses momentum. So now 'shuffle' the presentation a little so that you get the variety you are looking for.

Stage Three

Once the presentation is over, collect 'feed-back' and note it onto your story board. Now use this feed-back for future presentations.

THREE EXAMPLES

1. Team meeting. *Use the 'story-board' to keep 'ringing the changes', noticing what works and equally what doesn't work.*

SEVEN QUICK WAYS TO IMPROVE AN INHERITED PRESENTATION

Many of us have to give the presentations of others. A slide deck provided 'by marketing'. The 'standard sales pitch'. 'HR's explanation of the new compensation scheme'. How do you make it your own?

1. Read it several times. If at all possible go back to the author/s for deeper explanation of what they were trying to get across. Five minute phone conversation.
2. Sketch out a 'storyboard': a square for every one minute of the presentation. One minute.
3. Write what is currently happening in the presentation every minute in the squares. It's likely to be 'slide', 'slide', slide'. One minute.
4. Think, consider, reflect. What could make the talk more powerful, interesting, engaging? Five minutes.
5. Now revise what will be happening in some of those minutes/squares. Five minutes.
6. Rehearse it.
7. Give it.

You're an even better presenter.

THE BIG SEVEN, NUMBER 6: STORYBOARD OR YOU ARE A FILM DIRECTOR

10

2. Training course. *Story boards are brilliant for training courses, allowing you to get easy insight and perspective on how to achieve what you wish to achieve at each section.*
3. Major conferences. *This is a brilliant way to avoid being sucked into the classic PowerPoint slide-deck.*

THE SURGERY IS OPEN

1. Err, what is the balance between plenty of variety and too much chopping and changing? *The easiest answer is experience. As you build your experience you will just 'know' what works well, what should follow something, what would be a great way to start or finish etc. Until that point, get good at reading the audience. If they are clearly restless you need more engagement which might be driven by change. But if they are looking a little bewildered, maybe you need to give them the comfort of being 'grounded' in the same topic or style for a while...*
2. Err, where can I get good ideas on how to create variety when putting together my storyboard? *Start with noticing what other presenters do which you enjoy. TV and films can prompt an idea. Review old storyboards from previous presentations and think what ideas could you give 'a twist' and which could you build upon and maybe be even bolder?*
3. Err, I have an impossible topic. It is so fact based, so boring. *Consider stripping out all the facts and ask people to pre-read before your session (say you will start with a quiz...). Then use the session for help in implementing the ideas and doing a Q&A.*

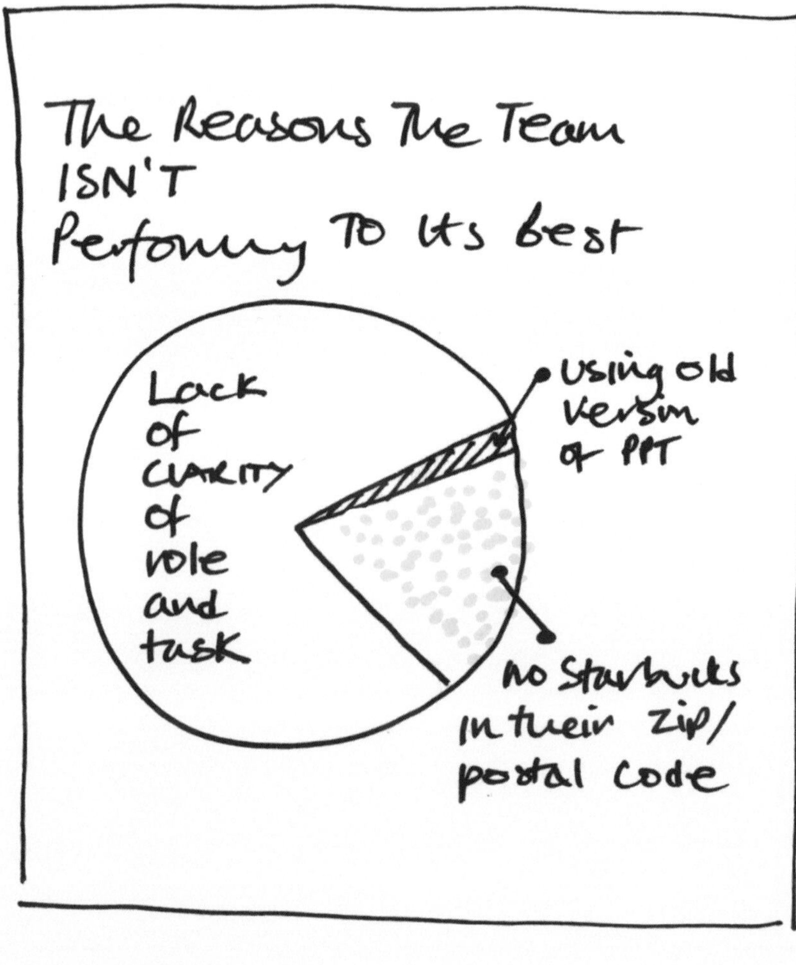
The Reasons The Team ISN'T Performing To its best
Lack of CLARITY of role and task
Using old Version of PPT
no Starbucks in their zip/postal code

THE BIG SEVEN, NUMBER SEVEN: SLIDES OR THE SLIDE IS NOT THE PRESENTATION

11

THE BIG IDEA

Do not START with the idea of slides; END with using some slides, maybe.

In one sense, that's it: that's all you need to know. The biggest mistake made by so many presenters, when given an assignment which *suggests* a possible presentation, is to immediately start typing into PowerPoint or to ask to 'borrow a slide-deck'. And is that a problem? Yes! It is (1) assuming a presentation is needed (2) assuming that slides will be the best way to get the message across. But perhaps both points are false? How do we avoid getting onto that mis-leading path?

Easy. Remember that slides are not the presentation; agreed, they are frequently used and they have become the norm. But they are not the presentation. Start instead with the outcome you want, the action, at the most fundamental level: when people leave the room following your session, what do you want them to do? Then create your storyboard matching to the seven-part structure (wow/agenda/connect/solution/Q&A/summary/action), making decisions as you work about appropriate state, space, story, structure, spikes... Now, as that planning comes to an end you will at times face a dilemma: there is no easy way to communicate the idea or concept. A story can't do it. An exercise can't do it. But you realise that a visual or a slide can do it. Hey presto: the storyboard flushes out what is required, in particular it reveals when a slide, particularly a PowerPoint slide is needed.

PRESENTING TWO

If you only do two things:

1. Reduce your number of slides by 50%.
2. Be absolutely definitely clear on what you want your audience to walk away with.

THE BIG SEVEN, NUMBER SEVEN: SLIDES OR THE SLIDE IS NOT THE PRESENTATION

11

Here are some examples of where a slide may well be useful:

- Facts & Figures. This certainly seems a natural choice. However, consider whether perhaps just the key figure/s can be pulled out and talked about. Thus rather than a whole slide which reproduces an entire excel spreadsheet, pluck out the essential figures on 'fall in customer satisfaction' and weave a story around that.
- Visual of something which cannot be shown in any other way. It is better to show the new fabric or phone. But if it can't, a picture is great.
- A quotation. "make a dent in the Universe", Steve Jobs. But don't read it.
- Flow diagrams for sequences or methodologies.

Finally, let us express a subtle point which is often lost. When we do a presentation, we (the presenter) essentially need three things. One: our own notes, our own road-map. We now understand that to be the story-board which is for our eyes only. Then we may need some visuals to help express ideas, to help keep the audience on-track. And finally of course we may want to leave the audience with some summary materials, some notes. For so many presenters, all three are put together, are literally merged in a PowerPoint slide-deck presentation. If you do this it is worth bearing in mind that you will probably do all three badly:

The irony of the INTENSE internal branding session was that all PPT slides now...

looked identical.

GOOD FOR TRANCE
BAD FOR ENGAGEMENT

THE BIG SEVEN, NUMBER SEVEN: SLIDES OR THE SLIDE IS NOT THE PRESENTATION

11

1. If you have excellent notes (i.e. close to verbatim) on the screen and thus on the slide-deck you are effectively 'giving away' your presentation: the audience can race ahead of you. They can ask you to skip, for example. They can be impatient.

2. You will end up giving away as a hand-out the presentation, the journey i.e. the sequence of slides, not the destination which is what they want and what you want them to act upon.

3. As a summary format, PowerPoint is not that great. It appears great, because it is in bite-sized bullets. But what people really want is the connections; the joined-up thinking. That's word. Word has joined up thinking, not fragmented thinking.

HOW TO DO IT

1. Write a SMART objective for the piece of communication (presumably to a group) to whom you are about to communicate.

2. Decide the best method or methods for that communication.

3. If one of those is a presentation, use a storyboard to manage your seven-step structure (the 'what') and then how you will do that.

4. If you have no other way to provide an excellent communication, then maybe a PowerPoint slide would be useful.

SEVEN WAYS TO CONNECT WITH YOUR AUDIENCE

1. **Ask questions, especially rhetorical**... *so why do I keep emphasising the importance of defending price...?*
2. **Make it sensory rich**. Tell your story with detail. *How late was your plane? How valuable was the business?*
3. **Less is more. Make what you do say valuable to your specific audience**. *So thus, in your company that would be a saving of $5.5/head...*
4. **Connect with early arrivals**. Get in the room early and greet as many people as you can.
5. **Talk from the back of the room, too**. Make sure you have a roving mike and can include all areas of the room.
6. **Keep to time**. Breaks and close.
7. **Respect every one in the audience**, even those who apparently are being 'difficult'. Handle then assertively not aggressively.

THE BIG SEVEN, NUMBER SEVEN: SLIDES OR THE SLIDE IS NOT THE PRESENTATION

11

THREE EXAMPLES

1. Team meeting. *Don't use slides. Simply e-mail an 'executive summary' with action points of what is required.*
2. Training course. *Create a 'work-book' which allows people to concentrate, to jot a few notes and to stay engaged, but NOT be able to 'read ahead'.*
3. Major conferences. *Talk 'unplugged' a lot more. For those who wish for a record of what you have said direct them to a downloadable-say-PDF of what has been said held on your blog.*

THE SURGERY IS OPEN

1. Err... what about the expectation that I should be using PowerPoint?
   It is a strong expectation. But there will be no difficulty at all if you deliver to your objective.

2. Err... what about handouts? A slide-deck is so convenient. *It is. But it's rarely a good hand-out unless you put all the words on the slide in which case you're adding little value and you have to consider why it is a presentation in the first place!*

3. Err... so you are saying present without a reminder of what to say?
   No. You need to practise and you need notes. Simply don't share them with your audience.

WHAT GOES WRONG AT CONFERENCES

A lot goes really well, but conference organisers could make it a lot easier for their audience if:

They did less. In the quest to keep people interested many organisers pack in a lot of speakers. No; what you need are *fewer speakers and ensure they are really good.*

They did more. Too often conferences are like the worst of politicians: all sound-bite and no action. Create a method for *capturing agreed actions and reporting one month after the event on progress.*

They DIDN'T start the previous evening. Typically people fly in–late–from all over the world. They hit the bar. Day one at 09.00 is not pretty sight. Start at 11.00 day one. Do 2h then lunch etc etc. *It means a day's alcohol free work is pretty well guaranteed.*

They forget the freebies. Special folders, bags and T-shirts have zero long-term use. Save that money and the money from starting on day one rather than the previous evening and invest it in something that really wins business.

They took the post conference feed-back seriously and didn't get all defensive about it.

HOW TO GET REALLY GOOD AT PRESENTING. INCLUDING TIMING & NOTES 12

How do you get really, really good at presenting? The answer is practice. Get up on your feet in front of people so that you become truly great at the craft. Why does it work:

- It changes the threshold of fear. We fear presenting for so many reasons. What will people think? Will there be tricky questions? Will they like my ideas? Will I have enough material? It will always remain. It needs to remain. But the more you practise, the more you can expect two things. One that the amount of fear will reduce. And secondly, that once you start speaking it will diminish quickly. These are very good reasons for practising a lot.
- It builds presentation 'mental muscle memory'. The more you stand up in front of people the more the skills which you need to manage groups such as good eye contact, moving to the side of a room with a large audience, supporting your words with positive body language become 'wired in' so that you do them unconsciously: you become unconsciously competent.
- It allows accelerated learning. The more you present, the more you learn what works for you. You're a great story teller perhaps, or you're good with high-energy 'things to do' lists. Or...
- It encourages you to seek self-awareness. The more you present, the more you can 'switch off' 'scared' reptile brain and 'switch on' thinking human brain. And once that brain is engaged you can notice what you are doing and improve...

Scannable PPT slides
no audience necessary

HOW TO GET REALLY GOOD AT PRESENTING. INCLUDING TIMING & NOTES 12

So if it is so brilliant, why don't people do it? Practise that is?

- Apparent lack of time. Once you become a serious presenter you realise that it's not just 'do' as in doing the presentation, it is 'plan-do-review' I.e. you put aside some time to plan the presentation. You do the presentation and then you review it. Arrggh "I haven't got time for that, they say". Arrggh but you haven't got time not to... if you wish the actions to be realised.
- Unsure what to do. The mistake of endless rehearsal. It perhaps seems obvious the business of rehearsal. But, it's not just a mindless 'going through' the notes hoping it will stick. No it's about articulation. It's about stating those words out aloud enough times so that when you are up in front of an audience 'you have been there before'.

This is a good point to talk about timing and notes.

- Timing. A professional presenter hits the correct time. He/she does not over-run. He/she does not finish early. Meant to finish speaking at 11.00? then at 10.59 they thank their audience and leave the stage. How do they do it?
    - Component 1: they know their presentation and its length as a consequence of having rehearsed a couple of times.
    - Component 2: they have some material they can add. They have some material they can drop. Neither of these actions should be apparent to the audience. And if they are necessary they should not be mentioned to an audience: the action of 'editing' material may worry an audience that they haven't had their 'money's worth'.

12 WAYS TO MAKE YOUR PRESENTATION MORE INTERESTING AND MORE FUN FOR THE AUDIENCE

1. Get into the room early and work out how you can get physically closer to the audience.
2. Remove as many distractions as possible: posters in the audience eye–line, for example.
3. Remove all obvious sense of time e.g. a clock above your head.
4. 1/3 into your presentation use a story to reinforce the points you are making.
5. 2/3 into your presentation change media e.g. from PowerPoint to whiteboard.
6. Do the Q & A before the summary.
7. Start on time. Yes, even though many people are late. Reward the behaviours you seek.
8. Finish on time. If you continue to talk, you many have them physically, but certainly not mentally.
9. Read Presenting101 on my blog.
10. Stay in control: do not let someone asking questions remove your leadership position.
11. As soon as you finish and the room clears, write your own personal review: what went well? And less well?
12. Plan your presentation to meet your outcome, not to fill the time available with PowerPoint slides.

HOW TO GET REALLY GOOD AT PRESENTING. INCLUDING TIMING & NOTES

12

- Component 3. A clear time-piece which is visible only to you. A clear clock on a desk is ideal. But if at all possible, remove all clocks from your presenting space. The glimpse of a clock takes people out of your world, out of the space you are creating which is dedicated solely to your message.
- Component 4. A practised eye which is able to scan between the audience notes and timepiece whilst giving the appearance that the audience is getting all of the attention.

- Notes. A professional presenter does not read from a script. They have a compelling conversation with the audience. Sure it is one-sided conversation. But for the audience it should feel as if they are being spoken with rather than spoken at. How is that achieved?
  - Become familiar with your materials. Your only knowledge of the subject matter should not be just what is on the slides.
  - Articulate what you are going to say several times. So that you have been there before.
  - Practise getting into a flow state i.e. extended periods without notes.
  - Write notes as key sentences (not key words) and which are written in large letters so that they can be seen from a distance.

Vipul (age 5¾) had been <u>really</u> enjoying his trip to the zoo until he discovered he needed to create a PPT slide-deck on his 'experiences'.

Little did he realise...

POWERPOINT IS NOT WORD. BULLETS ARE NOT NARRATIVE.

13

PowerPoint generates slides and slides generate slide-decks. And slide-decks without the presenter (even sometimes with the presenter!) generate confusion. A slide-deck is not a narrative. Very often there is insufficient logical build-up: the story is missing.

If you are dependent on people understanding and interpreting from a handout there is a far better piece of software: that is word. Word ensures the use of sentences which build to paragraphs which lead to understanding. The classic executive summary should not be dead yet.

Once again we are reminded of the dangers of going straight to PowerPoint to create our presentation. If we create from a clear objective, supported by a story-board we will produce what is necessary which will probably mean full supporting materials.

QUESTIONS IN PRESENTATIONS

If there is a fear beyond the fear of giving the presentation, there is the fear of taking *questions during the presentation*. And yet I would suggest questions from the audience to you are essential for two reasons: (1) the nature and number of the questions you receive correlates closely with the buy-in and understanding of the audience i.e. have you done what you were there for? And (2) it causes you to think on your feet and raise your game–a natural accelerator for developing your best presenting skills.

So perhaps rather than planning to dissuade questions, plan to encourage them by:

Being in the room to meet those who arrive early so people discover you are approachable and happy to take a query or two.

In long presentations having a mid-session pause where you allow people a minute or two to review what had gone so far and raise any issues.

Allow enough time for a full Q&A.

'Seeding' quieter audiences by mentioning questions from previous sessions.

Thanking those who question you to encourage others.

WHY THE DESIRE TO CREATE A 'PRESENTATION EXPERIENCE' IS MISTAKEN 14

It is possible to say of the theatre or the circus that one is seeking an experience. Something memorable, thought-provoking and up-lifting. But this is not what is important in business although it has become the new aspiration. In a world of over-load it is thought that the way to create impact is via the 'experience'. However, too much of an emotional 'vibe' can simply distract from the forward motion which is necessary to run the business. Too much discussion of how wonderful the music was can distract from the new product client benefits. The clowns were superb but they make the men's shirts being launched seem dull.

Clearly we wish our audience to feel good, to feel motivated and to have positive associations. But this is best done by sheer professionalism. By a relevant message. By clear help for the sales force. Rather than empty theatricals.

Nelson's slide-deck from Trafalgar, 1805 discovered at bottom of old chest.

VISUAL AIDS COMPARED 15

Of course, the classic 'visual aid' is now PowerPoint; in fact the term 'visual aid' sounds a little dated and comes from a time when presenters did consider the best tool for the job rather than just assuming 'it must be PowerPoint'. This piece of software is so ubiquitous it is now the presentation. And that makes things interesting for you. Assuming you've got the content (what you are going to say) to the best format possible, the way that you say it could make a dramatic difference. If you go the PowerPoint route you'll be like 97% of other presenters. But. But... If you decide to do something a little different you will already be standing out. And as we have said many time with presenting: that is no bad thing at all.

So:

You. That's you unplugged.

The format: just you and maybe a microphone. No support in any format.

The upside: as you gain experience you can become infinitely flexible. You can go slower, faster, louder, deeper. You can change style or topic. You can address issues. You can engage with the audience, you can integrate their topics. You appear highly credible. You can make the whole presentation a perfect match for the audience as it is customised 'on the fly'. Timing should be perfect as nobody is aware of what you intended to cover. There is nothing technical nor mechanical to go wrong.

ADD SPARK TO YOUR PRESENTATION

1. Make it more local: totally relevant to your audience.
2. Give it extra pace: keep them engaged.
3. Add some hard, undeniable facts: shock them.
4. Add perspective: why is this vital?
5. Make it clear: articulate well by practising.
6. Add drama through a story: have them begging for more.
7. Give a clear call for action so they felt their time was well spent.

VISUAL AIDS COMPARED 15

The downside: it helps tremendously to have experience and so it is best to use this in small doses in otherwise more structured and supported presentations. But don't let that put you off. Just a bit of 'unplugged' done well with the audience is brilliantly effective and certainly appreciated by those listening. And it is great for developing your confidence.

PowerPoint
The upside: a complete support structure, notes, prompts everything. You're unlikely to be at a loss for words. And so often it is 'expected' that you will have taken this approach. So nobody can 'complain'.

The downside: it's increasingly difficult to deliver a really good one. And you'll need to be really good if you are say at a conference embedded amongst other PowerPoint presenters.

Other Hi tech e.g. embedded video
Up side: A potentially very smooth reinforcement to what you have been talking about: *"let's now hear from Mrs Smith, one of our early customers, now...*

Downside: Often are clearly not a true part of the presentation and have actually been included to 'increase interest'. Often far too long.

Flip-chart
Up-side: Nicely low-tech. Allows a record to be kept. Can be pre-prepared in pencil and of course whole pages can be pre-prepared.

THE SIMPLE STUFF OF GREAT PRESENTATIONS

1. Start on time. Whatever.
2. Finish on time. Whatever.
3. Be clear on your goal in presenting. And get it, whatever.
4. Make it easy, really easy to understand.
5. Be enthusiastic about the topic.
6. Remove all distractions be it stale sandwiches or bleeping phones.
7. Thank your audience.

VISUAL AIDS COMPARED 15

Down-side: Can look very 'scruffy'. Can be too small for a larger audience.

White-board: as with flip-chart. Some are of courses available which will print what you have written or of course you could just take a photo as a record with your phone.

Henry Ford Gets It Across.

CRISES: HANDLING PROBLEMS 16

Crises are bad enough any time; they are certainly no fun when twenty people are watching you. Here are some tips:

When you have completed your preparation and there is nothing more to do apart from practise, put on a 'detached' or 'external observer' mindset and review every aspect of your talk looking at what could go wrong. And then create a Plan B.

How far do your plan for every eventuality? That is for you to decide and weighing up the risk of things going wrong and the consequences of not being able to proceed. If your laptop in your regular team meeting breaks down then it's probably no big deal. But if it fails at the sales conference, how quickly can you switch to an alternative delivery mechanism? Or does it mean the product briefing to fifty salespeople cannot go ahead? Presumably not. So, how quickly can the difficulty be solved?

Problems are best handled by a two-pronged approach of anticipation i.e. planning ahead. E.g. it should be enough that you can get access to the room at 09.00 for a 10.00 kick-off. But how about if you got there at 08.30: that gives 30 minutes of extra time to discover that the air-con simply isn't working. And knowing who to speak to if there is a problem.

Problems with people in the session are best handled firstly by knowing who will be in the audience you are talking to and what they are expecting. If you give people what they want and deliver it in a professional manner it makes the next

THE SEVEN POTENTIALLY PROBLEMATIC P-FACTORS WITH POWERPOINT

1. Paralysis. The state of deep trance induced by a mind-numbingly unimaginative, script-laden and over-full slide-deck.
2. PowerPoint Pareto Number. The number of slides to which the typical corporate slide-deck should be reduced for normal human consumption. Research suggests 20% of the original.
3. PowerPoint Paradigm. The bizarre fact that the greater the 'whizziness' of the presentation model the more the point of the presentation is lost.
4. PowerPoint Pointer. The simple laser device used in hi-tech presentations to replace the old music hall sing-along bouncing ball as everybody reads the script together.
5. PowerPoint Punchline. *"...and as with everybody else this morning, I have way too many slides. I am sorry about the fact that many of the colours are a poor choice for this bright sun-light... oh, there we go... not sure why the embedded video is not working... haha..."*
6. PowerPoint Panchakarma. The ancient Indian system of Ayurveda detox which is essential if the average PowerPoint user is ever going to be able to learn how to communicate again in the real world.
7. PowerPoint Primate. The monkey who would keep it simple, keep it engaging and undoubtedly get the message across in less time. Because thankfully they haven't learnt PowerPoint yet. But they know how to have a good time.

stage easier. And that is being assertive with people who are being unreasonable or who are dominating your session. Remember when in a large forum, everyone has to compromise: it is your duty as leader of the session to remind them of that. But do it with courtesy: never damage a relationship, especially in a public forum. You might find one of my other books helpful on this topic of dealing with people assertively: *'Have It Your Way'*, ISBN: 1905940467.

WE MISS THE (POWER)POINT

You've probably noticed a trend amongst conference organisers to start saying 'no PowerPoint' or 'no more than three PowerPoint slides'.

Poor thinking. When PowerPoint became available, teachers, lecturers and anyone who stood up to talk to an audience was expected to use the software. Why? because (apparently) it made them professional. That's what we wanted: professional presenting. Then the art of talking to an audience was lost as people become too involved in the technology so that now PowerPoint is synonymous with dull, 'reading off the screen'... But of course it needn't be.

Refuse to follow any guidelines about PowerPoint. But insist on giving a great, interesting stimulating talk. Which may or may not include PowerPoint slides.

BACK TO BASICS: A SUMMARY AND HOW TO PRODUCE THE DEFINITIVE PRESENTATION IN NINE EASY STEPS 17

As with most great pieces of work, a fantastic presentation is produced by doing work fully, consistently and early. Never leave putting a presentation together to the last minute; the pain is too much!

Thus **Step 1**: has to be '*Why am I doing this presentation?*'. And this in itself has **two** aspects. Firstly: What do I want to accomplish? What is the action I seek of my audience? And secondly: why do I want to use the format of a presentation? Would a quick phone call to a couple of the decision-makers do the job as well or even better? Be aware of being 'asked to do a presentation'; there may well be a better format.

Step 2: if you are not already, get immersed in the subject as much as time allows, so that if you are not already a 'subject matter expert', then you become as close to one as you can. Stay away from PowerPoint at this stage; it will simply distract from your clearest thinking. And if someone has kindly given you a PowerPoint slide-deck and said 'use this', consider it a bonus resource. But don't refer to it yet.

Conversely **Step 3**: if you do feel you are an expert in the subject, then get some perspective. Stay away from PowerPoint and/or cannibalised/former slide-decks. Ask yourself: if I were starting this afresh, how would I go about it?

Step 4: Remind yourself of the seven part structure and prepare your material around the *wow/agenda/connect/solution/Q&A/summary/action* process. Concentrate on what you are going to say. If supporting material, and or presentation ideas come to mind, jot them down; but do not dwell on them for the moment.

THE AUDIENCE IS ALWAYS ON YOUR SIDE

If:

1. You are clearly prepared.
2. You have worked hard to make it relevant to them specifically.
3. You're enthusiastic and keen. But not full of yourself.
4. You can minimise and manage the questions from those who like the sound of their own voice.
5. You didn't just read PowerPoint slides to them. You had some anecdotes and illustrations.
6. You kept to time and agenda and purpose.
7. You were available for a few 1 to 1s at the end.

BACK TO BASICS: A SUMMARY AND HOW TO PRODUCE THE DEFINITIVE PRESENTATION IN NINE EASY STEPS

17

Step 5: Do a very rough, 'quick & dirty' rehearsal. How long did it last? Get a good 'synch' between the time you need to speak for and your materials. Now make sure you have some buffer (extra) material in case you run out of time. And know what you can edit/drop if you are taking too long.

Step 6: Now start storyboarding. Start with your action (7), then go back to the wow(1) and work though the rest of the stages (2–6) in order. You have your what (the words, the content), you are now thinking about how. Now take a look at any slide-decks that you have been offered. Any good ideas? Or good slides which you can use to augment your already great presentation.

Step 7: Now do a couple of final rehearsals, ideally in the room in which you will finally run your session. Ensure the mechanics of the **what** (you are going to say) and the **how** (you are going to say it) are seamlessly inter-woven.

Step 8: On the day, get to the room early. Pace a bit, practising your opening words.

Step 9: Run the session and collect feed-back to enable you to improve future sessions.

12 WAYS TO MAKE YOUR PRESENTATION MORE IMPACTFUL

1. Get into the room early and work out how you can get physically closer to the audience.
2. Remove as many distractions as possible: posters in the audience eye-line, for example.
3. Remove all obvious sense of time e.g. a clock above your head.
4. 1/3 into your presentation use a story to reinforce the points you are making.
5. 2/3 into your presentation change media e.g. from PowerPoint to whiteboard.
6. Do the Q & A before the summary.
7. Start on time. Yes, even though many people are late. Reward the behaviours you seek.
8. Finish on time. If you continue to talk, you many have them physically, but certainly not mentally.
9. Check through any hand-outs so that you are sure they are perfect.
10. Stay in control: do not let someone asking questions remove your leadership position.
11. As soon as you finish and the room clears, write your own personal review: what went well? And less well?
12. Plan your presentation to meet your outcome, not to fill the time available with PowerPoint slides.

NICHOLAS BATE

Nicholas Bate is passionate about supporting people to ensure they realise and release their true and full potential.

After a career in sales and marketing in the IT industry, culminating in leading sector marketing for Research Machines, Oxford, Nicholas launched Strategic Edge. A small, premium consultancy, Strategic Edge specialises in creating long-term competitive advantage for its clients by addressing individual performance. His clients include Barclays Bank, BBC, Marks & Spencer, Microsoft, MSN, Warwick Business School amongst others.

He is author, designer and facilitator for the groundbreaking 'Personal Excellence' seminar, a programme used as the basis for cultural change in many organisations, in addition to many pioneering development concepts in leadership, team building and sales training.

He is the author of nine acclaimed books:
Being The Best; how to realise and release your true potential
Instant MBA MBA thinking without the programme
Have it your Way: practical, everyday negotiation
Beat the Recession: a practical tool-kit for avoiding disaster
Get A Life: how to achieve the work-life balance you are seeking
JfDI: Just Do It: the definitive guide to enabling your vision
Unplugged: the time for personal re-invention is now
Blackberry Fool: how to use the device sensibly
Selling and Marketing in This Recession: great, instant strategies

IN 20

1. We only present to get action.
2. Seriously. Think about it. That's why you are in the room together: to get ACTION.
3. So that's where you start:
4. *What action do I want of these people when I have finished?*
5. To buy from me? Vote me in as President? Accept the redundancy package? Give me the job?
6. Now become a film director. How do you take them from where they are to taking that action?
7. You need a set of experiences: a powerful set of figures perhaps, a moving story maybe. An exercise. You decide.
8. A story board will help you: draw a matrix of boxes. One for every 90 seconds.
9. What will happen in that period of time to hold their interest? Write it in the box.
10. Think about your energy. Your energy level is infectious. High or Low.
11. Help them to understand e.g. stories, analogies, exercises.
12. And worry less about remembering what to say by putting your notes on a slide.
13. Use the space: get closer to your audience.
14. Use the leadership position of standing more often.
15. Build in spikes. Rhetorical questions. Louder. Quieter. Quick video. Quick exercise. Build the pace.
16. You need notes. Write them large for you only.
17. They need notes. Provide a word executive summary.
18. You need some visuals. OK possibly some PowerPoint slides.
19. But don't write everything in PowerPoint and give it out. They will read ahead, get bored, distracted and wonder.
20. Why are you there? See 1.

NICHOLAS BATE

Plus a range of 'mini-books' including:
Rules of Life; 14 Rules for Radicals; Blackberry Fool;
How To Think Like; Morph!; Boost your Productivity; LifeBalance, Outrageous101, Professional101, Celeb Productivity, A to Z of Excellence. A to Z of Sales Excellence...

Three specialist books are only available on-line through www.blurb.com/bookstore. These are 'How To Think Like...', '101' and 'The Beatles'. Go to the site to be able to view the books.

He is a visiting lecturer on the Warwick University Full-time and IBM MBA. Nicholas carried out research in the field of Molecular Biophysics at Magdalen College, Oxford University and is an NLP Master Practitioner, MBTI (levels 1 and 2) accredited and a qualified (PGCE) teacher. As well as instigating the Strategic Edge research programme, he has spent time studying with many of the recognised practitioners in the fields of business and personal development.

Nicholas's Blog **www.nicholasbate.typepad.com** has a world-wide following.

THE SIMPLE STUFF OF GREAT PRESENTATIONS SEVEN

1. Start on time. Whatever.
2. Finish on time. Whatever.
3. Be clear on your goal in presenting. And get it, whatever.
4. Make it easy, really easy to understand.
5. Be enthusiastic about the topic.
6. Remove all distractions be it stale sandwiches or bleeping phones.
7. Thank your audience.